Foreword

MW01202138

This book contains a set of 196 Geography Flash Cards.

These Flash Cards contain each areas flag, capital city, estimated population and the name of their currency.

The cards are presented in book form, so the user must cut the cards along the black line for the student to use them as cards.

When printing the flash cards in this book it is important to not duplex or two side print the pages. There are 4 cards per page.

Enjoy.....

World Geography Card

Afghanistan

Capital: Kabul
Est. Population:
31,056,997
Currency: Afghani

Country Card C1001

World Geography Card

Albania

Capital: Tiranë
Est. Population:
3,581,655
Currency: Lek

Country Card C1002

World Geography Card

Algeria

Capital: Algiers
Est. Population:
32,930,091
Currency: Dinar

Country Card C1003

World Geography Card

Andorra

Capital: Andorra la Vella
Est. Population:
71,201
Currency: Euro

Country Card C1004

World
Geography Card

Angola

Capital: Luanda
Est. Population:
12,127,071
Currency: New Kwanza

Country Card C1005

World
Geography
Card

Antigua and Barbuda

Capital: St. John's
Est. Population:
69,108
Currency: East
Caribbean dollar

Country Card C1006

World
Geography Card

<u>Argentina</u>

Capital: Buenos Aires
Est. Population: 39,921,833
Currency: Peso

Country Card C1007

World
Geography
Card

<u>Armenia</u>

Capital: Yerevan
Est. Population: 2,976,372
Currency: Dram

Country Card C1008

World
Geography
Card

Australia

Capital: Canberra
Est. Population:
20,264,082
Currency: Australian
dollar

Country Card C1009

World
Geography Card

Austria

Capital: Vienna
Est. Population:
8,192,880
Currency: Euro

Country Card C1010

World
Geography
Card

Azerbaijan

Capital: Baku
Est. Population:
7,961,619
Currency: Manat

Country Card C1011

World
Geography Card

Bahamas

Capital: Nassau
Est. Population:
303,770
Currency: Bahamian
dollar

Country Card C1012

World
Geography
Card

Bahrain

Capital: Al-Manámah
Est. Population:
698,585
Currency: Bahrain
dinar

Country Card C1013

World
Geography
Card

Bangladesh

Capital: Dhaka
Est. Population:
147,365,352
Currency: Taka

Country Card C1014

World
Geography
Card

Barbados

Capital: Bridgetown
Est. Population:
279,912
Currency: Barbados
dollar

Country Card C1015

World
Geography
Card

Belarus

Capital: Mensk (Minsk)
Est. Population:
10,293,011
Currency: Belorussian
ruble

Country Card C1016

World Geography Card

Belgium

Capital: Brussels
Est. Population:
10,379,067
Currency: Euro

Country Card C1017

World Geography Card

Belize

Capital: Belmopan
Est. Population:
287,730
Currency: Belize dollar

Country Card C1018

World Geography Card

Benin

Capital: Porto-Novo
Est. Population:
7,862,944
Currency: CFA Franc

Country Card C1019

World Geography Card

Bhutan

Capital: Thimphu
Est. Population:
2,279,723
Currency: Ngultrum

Country Card C1020

World
Geography
Card

Bolivia

Capital: La Paz
Est. Population:
8,989,046
Currency: Boliviano

Country Card C1021

World
Geography
Card

Bosnia and Herzegovina

Capital: Sarajevo
Est. Population:
4,498,976
Currency: Marka

Country Card C1022

World
Geography
Card

Botswana

Capital: Gaborone
Est. Population:
1,639,833
Currency: Pula

Country Card C1023

World
Geography
Card

Brazil

Capital: Brasília
Est. Population:
188,078,227
Currency: Real

Country Card C1024

World Geography Card

Brunei

Capital: Bandar Seri Begawan
Est. Population: 379,444
Currency: Brunei dollar

Country Card C1025

World Geography Card

Bulgaria

Capital: Sofia
Est. Population: 7,385,367
Currency: Lev

Country Card C1026

World Geography Card

Burkina Faso

Capital: Ouagadougou
Est. Population: 13,902,972
Currency: CFA Franc

Country Card C1027

World Geography Card

Burundi

Capital: Bujumbura
Est. Population: 8,090,068
Currency: Burundi franc

Country Card C1028

World
Geography
Card

Cambodia

Capital: Phnom Penh
Est. Population:
13,881,427
Currency: Riel

Country Card C1029

World
Geography
Card

Cameroon

Capital: Yaoundé
Est. Population:
17,340,702
Currency: CFA Franc

Country Card C1030

World
Geography
Card

Canada

Capital: Ottawa
Est. Population:
35,540,400
Currency: Canadian
dollar

Country Card C1031

World
Geography
Card

Cape Verde

Capital: Praia
Est. Population:
420,979
Currency: Cape
Verdean escudo

Country Card C1032

World
Geography
Card

Central African Republic

Capital: Bangui
Est. Population:
4,303,356
Currency: CFA Franc

Country Card C1033

World
Geography Card

Chad

Capital: N'Djamena
Est. Population:
9,944,201
Currency: CFA Franc

Country Card C1034

World
Geography
Card

Chile

Capital: Santiago
Est. Population:
16,134,219
Currency: Chilean Peso

Country Card C1035

World
Geography Card

China

Capital: Beijing
Est. Population:
1,313,973,713
Currency:
Yuan/Renminbi

Country Card C1036

World
Geography
Card

Colombia

Capital: Bogotá
Est. Population:
43,593,035
Currency: Colombian
Peso

Country Card C1037

World
Geography
Card

Comoros

Capital: Moroni
Est. Population:
690,948
Currency: Franc

Country Card C1038

World
Geography
Card

Democratic Republic of the Congo

Capital: Brazzaville
Est. Population:
3,702,314
Currency: Congolese
franc

Country Card C1039

World
Geography
Card

Congo, Republic of

Capital: Kinshasa
Est. Population:
62,660,551
Currency: CFA Franc

Country Card C1040

World Geography Card

Costa Rica

Capital: San José
Est. Population:
4,075,261
Currency: Colón

Country Card C1041

World Geography Card

Côte d'Ivoire

Capital: Yamoussoukro
Est. Population:
17,654,843
Currency: CFA Franc

Country Card C1042

World Geography Card

Croatia

Capital: Zagreb
Est. Population:
4,494,749
Currency: Kuna

Country Card C1043

World Geography Card

Cuba

Capital: Havana
Est. Population:
11,382,820
Currency: Cuban Peso

Country Card C1044

World
Geography
Card

Cyprus

Capital: Nicosia
Est. Population:
784,301
Currency: Cyprus
pound

Country Card C1045

World
Geography
Card

Czech Republic

Capital: Prague
Est. Population:
10,235,455
Currency: Koruna

Country Card C1046

World
Geography
Card

Denmark

Capital: Copenhagen
Est. Population:
5,450,661
Currency: Krone

Country Card C1047

World
Geography
Card

Djibouti

Capital: Djibouti
Est. Population:
486,530
Currency: Djibouti
franc

Country Card C1048

World
Geography
Card

Dominica

Capital: Roseau
Est. Population: 68,910
Currency: East
Caribbean dollar

Country Card C1049

World
Geography Card

Dominican Republic

Capital: Santo Domingo
Est. Population:
9,183,984
Currency: Dominican
Peso

Country Card C1050

World
Geography
Card

East Timor

Capital: Dili
Est. Population:
1,062,777
Currency: U.S. dollar

Country Card C1051

World
Geography Card

Ecuador

Capital: Quito
Est. Population:
13,547,510
Currency: U.S. dollar

Country Card C1052

Egypt

Capital: Cairo
Est. Population:
78,887,007
Currency: Egyptian
pound

Country Card C1053

El Salvador

Capital: San Salvador
Est. Population:
6,822,378
Currency: Colón; U.S.
dollar

Country Card C1054

Equatorial Guinea

Capital: Malabo
Est. Population:
540,109
Currency: CFA Franc

Country Card C1055

Eritrea

Capital: Asmara
Est. Population:
4,786,994
Currency: Nakfa

Country Card C1056

World
Geography
Card

Estonia

Capital: Tallinn
Est. Population:
1,324,333
Currency: Kroon

Country Card C1057

World
Geography Card

Ethiopia

Capital: Addis Ababa
Est. Population:
74,777,981
Currency: Birr

Country Card C1058

World
Geography
Card

Fiji

Capital: Suva
Est. Population:
905,949
Currency: Fiji dollar

Country Card C1059

World
Geography Card

Finland

Capital: Helsinki
Est. Population:
5,231,372
Currency: Euro
(formerly markka)

Country Card C1060

France

Capital: Paris
Est. Population:
60,876,136
Currency: Euro
(formerly French franc)

Country Card C1061

Gabon

Capital: Libreville
Est. Population:
1,424,906
Currency: CFA Franc

Country Card C1062

Gambia

Capital: Banjul
Est. Population:
1,641,564
Currency: Dalasi

Country Card C1063

Georgia

Capital: Tbilisi
Est. Population:
4,661,473
Currency: Lari

Country Card C1064

World
Geography
Card

Germany

Capital: Berlin
Est. Population:
82,422,299
Currency: Euro (formerly
Deutsche mark)

Country Card C1065

World
Geography Card

Ghana

Capital: Accra
Est. Population:
22,409,572
Currency: Cedi

Country Card C1066

World
Geography
Card

Greece

Capital: Athens
Est. Population:
10,688,058
Currency: Euro
(formerly drachma)

Country Card C1067

World
Geography Card

Grenada

Capital: St. George's
Est. Population: 89,703
Currency: East
Caribbean dollar

Country Card C1068

World
Geography
Card

Guatemala

Capital: Guatemala City
Est. Population: 12,293,545
Currency: Quetzal

Country Card C1069

World
Geography
Card

Guinea

Capital: Conakry
Est. Population: 9,690,222
Currency: Guinean franc

Country Card C1070

World
Geography
Card

Guinea-Bissau

Capital: Bissau
Est. Population: 1,442,029
Currency: CFA Franc

Country Card C1071

World
Geography
Card

Guyana

Capital: Georgetown
Est. Population: 767,245
Currency: Guyanese dollar

Country Card C1072

World Geography Card

Haiti

Capital: Port-au-Prince
Est. Population:
8,308,504
Currency: Gourde

Country Card C1073

World Geography Card

Honduras

Capital: Tegucigalpa
Est. Population:
7,326,496
Currency: Lempira

Country Card C1074

World Geography Card

Hungary

Capital: Budapest
Est. Population:
9,981,334
Currency: Forint

Country Card C1075

World Geography Card

Iceland

Capital: Reykjavik
Est. Population:
299,388
Currency: Icelandic króna

Country Card C1076

World Geography Card

India

Capital: New Delhi
Est. Population:
1,095,351,995
Currency: Rupee

Country Card C1077

World Geography Card

Indonesia

Capital: Jakarta
Est. Population:
245,452,739
Currency: Rupiah

Country Card C1078

World Geography Card

Iran

Capital: Tehran
Est. Population:
68,688,433
Currency: Rial

Country Card C1079

World Geography Card

Iraq

Capital: Baghdad
Est. Population:
26,783,383
Currency: U.S. dollar

Country Card C1080

World
Geography
Card

Ireland

Capital: Dublin
Est. Population:
4,062,235
Currency: Euro
(formerly Irish pound)

Country Card C1081

World
Geography Card

Israel

Capital: Jerusalem
Est. Population:
6,352,117
Currency: Shekel

Country Card C1082

World
Geography
Card

Italy

Capital: Rome
Est. Population:
58,133,509
Currency: Euro
(formerly lira)

Country Card C1083

World
Geography Card

Jamaica

Capital: Kingston
Est. Population:
2,758,124
Currency: Jamaican
dollar

Country Card C1084

World
Geography
Card

Japan

Capital: Tokyo
Est. Population:
127,463,611
Currency: Yen

Country Card C1085

World
Geography
Card

Jordan

Capital: Amman
Est. Population:
5,906,760
Currency: Jordanian
dinar

Country Card C1086

World
Geography
Card

Kazakhstan

Capital: Astana
Est. Population:
15,233,244
Currency: Tenge

Country Card C1087

World
Geography
Card

Kenya

Capital: Nairobi
Est. Population:
34,707,817
Currency: Kenya
shilling

Country Card C1088

World
Geography
Card

Kiribati

Capital: Tarawa
Est. Population:
105,432
Currency: Australian
dollar

Country Card C1089

World
Geography Card

Korea, North

Capital: Pyongyang
Est. Population:
23,113,019
Currency: Won

Country Card C1090

World
Geography
Card

Korea, South

Capital: Seoul
Est. Population:
48,846,823
Currency: Won

Country Card C1091

World
Geography Card

Kuwait

Capital: Kuwait City
Est. Population:
2,418,393
Currency: Kuwaiti
dinar

Country Card C1092

World Geography Card

Kyrgyzstan

Capital: Bishkek
Est. Population:
5,213,898
Currency: Som

Country Card C1093

World Geography Card

Laos

Capital: Vientiane
Est. Population:
6,368,481
Currency: New Kip

Country Card C1094

World Geography Card

Latvia

Capital: Riga
Est. Population:
2,274,735
Currency: Lats

Country Card C1095

World Geography Card

Lebanon

Capital: Beirut
Est. Population:
3,874,050
Currency: Lebanese pound

Country Card C1096

World
Geography
Card

Lesotho

Capital: Maseru
Est. Population:
2,022,331
Currency: Maluti

Country Card C1097

World
Geography Card

Liberia

Capital: Monrovia
Est. Population:
3,042,004
Currency: Liberian
dollar

Country Card C1098

World
Geography
Card

Libya

Capital: Tripoli
Est. Population:
5,900,754
Currency: Libyan
dinar

Country Card C1099

World
Geography Card

Liechtenstein

Capital: Vaduz
Est. Population: 33,987
Currency: Swiss franc

Country Card C1100

World Geography Card

Lithuania

Capital: Vilnius
Est. Population:
3,585,906
Currency: Litas

Country Card C1101

World Geography Card

Luxembourg

Capital: Luxembourg
Est. Population:
474,413
Currency: Euro (formerly Luxembourg franc)

Country Card C1102

World Geography Card

Macedonia

Capital: Skopje
Est. Population:
2,050,554
Currency: Denar

Country Card C1103

World Geography Card

Madagascar

Capital: Antananarivo
Est. Population:
18,595,469
Currency: Malagasy franc

Country Card C1104

World
Geography
Card

Malawi

Capital: Lilongwe
Est. Population:
13,013,926
Currency: Kwacha

Country Card C1105

World
Geography Card

Malaysia

Capital: Kuala Lumpur
Est. Population:
24,385,858
Currency: Ringgit

Country Card C1106

World
Geography
Card

Maldives

Capital: Malé
Est. Population:
359,008
Currency: Rufiya

Country Card C1107

World
Geography Card

Mali

Capital: Bamako
Est. Population:
11,716,829
Currency: CFA Franc

Country Card C1108

World Geography Card

Malta

Capital: Valletta
Est. Population: 400,214
Currency: Maltese lira

Country Card C1109

World Geography Card

Marshall Islands

Capital: Majuro
Est. Population: 60,422
Currency:

Country Card C1110

World Geography Card

Mauritania

Capital: Nouakchott
Est. Population: 3,177,388
Currency: Ouguiya

Country Card C1111

World Geography Card

Mauritius

Capital: Port Louis
Est. Population: 1,240,827
Currency: Mauritian rupee

Country Card C1112

World Geography Card

Mexico

Capital: Mexico City
Est. Population: 107,449,525
Currency: Mexican peso

Country Card C1113

World Geography Card

Micronesia

Capital: Palikir
Est. Population: 108,004
Currency: US Dollar

Country Card C1114

World Geography Card

Moldova

Capital: Chisinau
Est. Population: 4,466,706
Currency: Leu

Country Card C1115

World Geography Card

Monaco

Capital: Monaco
Est. Population: 32,543
Currency: Euro

Country Card C1116

World
Geography
Card

Mongolia

Capital: Ulan Bator
Est. Population:
2,832,224
Currency: Tugrik

Country Card C1117

World
Geography Card

Montenegro

Capital: Cetinje
Est. Population:
630,548
Currency: Euro

Country Card C1118

World
Geography
Card

Morocco

Capital: Rabat
Est. Population:
33,241,259
Currency: Dirham

Country Card C1119

World
Geography Card

Mozambique

Capital: Maputo
Est. Population:
19,686,505
Currency: Metical

Country Card C1120

World
Geography
Card

Myanmar

Capital: Rangoon
Est. Population:
47,382,633
Currency: Kyat

Country Card C1121

World
Geography Card

Namibia

Capital: Windhoek
Est. Population:
2,044,147
Currency: Namibian
dollar

Country Card C1122

World
Geography
Card

Nauru

Capital: Yaren
Est. Population: 13,287
Currency: Australian
dollar

Country Card C1123

World
Geography Card

Nepal

Capital: Kathmandu
Est. Population:
28,287,147
Currency: Nepalese
rupee

Country Card C1124

World Geography Card

Netherlands

Capital: Amsterdam
Est. Population:
16,491,461
Currency: Euro
(formerly guilder)

Country Card C1125

World Geography Card

New Zealand

Capital: Wellington
Est. Population:
4,076,140
Currency: New Zealand
dollar

Country Card C1126

World Geography Card

Nicaragua

Capital: Managua
Est. Population:
5,570,129
Currency: Gold
cordoba

Country Card C1127

World Geography Card

Niger

Capital: Niamey
Est. Population:
12,525,094
Currency: CFA Franc

Country Card C1128

World Geography Card

Nigeria

Capital: Abuja
Est. Population:
131,859,731
Currency: Naira

Country Card C1129

World Geography Card

Norway

Capital: Oslo
Est. Population:
4,610,820
Currency: Norwegian krone

Country Card C1130

World Geography Card

Oman

Capital: Muscat
Est. Population:
3,102,229
Currency: Omani rial

Country Card C1131

World Geography Card

Pakistan

Capital: Islamabad
Est. Population:
165,803,560
Currency: Pakistan rupee

Country Card C1132

World Geography Card

Palau

Capital: Koror
Est. Population: 20,579
Currency: U.S. dollar used

Country Card C1133

World Geography Card

No Flag

Palestinian State (proposed)

Capital: Undetermined
Est. Population:
Currency: New Israeli shekels, Jordanian dinars, U.S. dollars

Country Card C1134

World Geography Card

Panama

Capital: Panama City
Est. Population: 3,191,319
Currency: balboa; U.S. dollar

Country Card C1135

World Geography Card

Papua New Guinea

Capital: Port Moresby
Est. Population: 5,670,544
Currency: Kina

Country Card C1136

World
Geography
Card

Paraguay

Capital: Asunción
Est. Population:
6,506,464
Currency: Guaraní

Country Card C1137

World
Geography Card

Peru

Capital: Lima
Est. Population:
28,302,603
Currency: Nuevo sol
(1991)

Country Card C1138

World
Geography
Card

Philippines

Capital: Manila
Est. Population:
89,468,677
Currency: Peso

Country Card C1139

World
Geography Card

Poland

Capital: Warsaw
Est. Population:
38,536,869
Currency: Zloty

Country Card C1140

World
Geography
Card

Portugal

Capital: Lisbon
Est. Population:
10,605,870
Currency: Euro
(formerly escudo)

Country Card C1141

World
Geography
Card

Qatar

Capital: Doha
Est. Population:
885,359
Currency: Qatari riyal

Country Card C1142

World
Geography
Card

Romania

Capital: Bucharest
Est. Population:
22,303,552
Currency: Leu

Country Card C1143

World
Geography
Card

Russia

Capital: Moscow
Est. Population:
142,893,540
Currency: Ruble

Country Card C1144

World
Geography Card

Rwanda

Capital: Kigali
Est. Population:
8,648,248
Currency: Rwanda
franc

Country Card C1145

World
Geography Card

St. Kitts and Nevis

Capital: Basseterre
Est. Population: 39,129
Currency: East
Caribbean dollar

Country Card C1146

World
Geography
Card

St. Lucia

Capital: Castries
Est. Population:
168,458
Currency: East
Caribbean dollar

Country Card C1147

World
Geography Card

St. Vincent and
the Grenadines

Capital: Kingstown
Est. Population:
117,848
Currency: East
Caribbean dollar

Country Card C1148

World
Geography
Card

Samoa

Capital: Apia
Est. Population:
176,908
Currency: Tala

Country Card C1149

World
Geography
Card

San Marino

Capital: San Marino
Est. Population: 29,251
Currency: Euro

Country Card C1150

World
Geography
Card

São Tomé and Príncipe

Capital: São Tomé
Est. Population:
193,413
Currency: Dobra

Country Card C1151

World
Geography Card

Saudi Arabia

Capital: Riyadh
Est. Population:
27,019,731
Currency: Riyal

Country Card C1152

World
Geography
Card

Senegal

Capital: Dakar
Est. Population:
11,987,121
Currency: CFA Franc

Country Card C1153

World
Geography Card

Serbia

Capital: Belgrade
Est. Population:
9,396,411
Currency: Yugoslav
new dinar

Country Card C1154

World
Geography
Card

Seychelles

Capital: Victoria
Est. Population: 81,541
Currency: Seychelles
rupee

Country Card C1155

World
Geography Card

Sierra Leone

Capital: Freetown
Est. Population:
6,005,250
Currency: Leone

Country Card C1156

World
Geography
Card

Singapore

Capital: Singapore
Est. Population:
4,492,150
Currency: Singapore
dollar

Country Card C1157

World
Geography Card

Slovakia

Capital: Bratislava
Est. Population:
5,439,448
Currency: Koruna

Country Card C1158

World
Geography
Card

Slovenia

Capital: Ljubljana
Est. Population:
2,010,347
Currency: Slovenian
tolar

Country Card C1159

World
Geography
Card

Solomon Islands

Capital: Honiara
Est. Population:
552,438
Currency: Solomon
Islands dollar

Country Card C1160

World Geography Card

Somalia

Capital: Mogadishu
Est. Population:
8,863,338
    Currency: Somali
shilling

Country Card C1161

World Geography Card

South Africa

Capital: Pretoria
Est. Population:
44,187,637
    Currency: Rand

Country Card C1162

World Geography Card

Spain

Capital: Madrid
Est. Population:
40,397,842
    Currency: Euro
(formerly peseta)

Country Card C1163

World Geography Card

Sri Lanka

Capital: Colombo
Est. Population:
20,222,240
    Currency: Sri Lanka
rupee

Country Card C1164

World
Geography
Card

Sudan

Capital: Khartoum
Est. Population:
41,236,378
Currency: Dinar

Country Card C1165

World
Geography
Card

Suriname

Capital: Paramaribo
Est. Population:
439,117
Currency: Surinamese
dollar

Country Card C1166

World
Geography
Card

Swaziland

Capital: Mbabane
Est. Population:
1,136,334
Currency: Lilangeni

Country Card C1167

World
Geography
Card

Sweden

Capital: Stockholm
Est. Population:
9,016,596
Currency: Krona

Country Card C1168

World
Geography Card

Switzerland

Capital: Bern
Est. Population:
7,523,934
Currency: Swiss franc

Country Card C1169

World
Geography Card

Syria

Capital: Damascus
Est. Population:
18,881,361
Currency: Syrian
pound

Country Card C1170

World
Geography
Card

Taiwan

Capital: Taipei
Est. Population:
23,036,087
Currency: Taiwan
dollar

Country Card C1171

World
Geography Card

Tajikistan

Capital: Dushanbe
Est. Population:
7,320,815
Currency: somoni

Country Card C1172

World Geography Card

Tanzania

Capital: Dodoma
Est. Population:
37,445,392
Currency: Tanzanian shilling

Country Card C1173

World Geography Card

Thailand

Capital: Bangkok
Est. Population:
64,631,595
Currency: baht

Country Card C1174

World Geography Card

Togo

Capital: Lomé
Est. Population:
5,548,702
Currency: CFA Franc

Country Card C1175

World Geography Card

Tonga

Capital: Nuku'alofa
Est. Population:
114,689
Currency: Pa'anga

Country Card C1176

World
Geography
Card

Trinidad and Tobago

Capital: Port-of-Spain
Est. Population:
1,065,842
Currency: Trinidad
and Tobago dollar

Country Card C1177

World
Geography Card

Tunisia

Capital: Tunis
Est. Population:
10,175,014
Currency: Tunisian
dinar

Country Card C1178

World
Geography
Card

Turkey

Capital: Ankara
Est. Population:
70,413,958
Currency: Turkish lira
(YTL)

Country Card C1179

World
Geography Card

Turkmenistan

Capital: Ashgabat
Est. Population:
5,042,920
Currency: Manat

Country Card C1180

World Geography Card

Tuvalu

Capital: Funafuti
Est. Population: 11,810
Currency: Australian dollar

Country Card C1181

World Geography Card

Uganda

Capital: Kampala
Est. Population: 28,195,754
Currency: Ugandan new shilling

Country Card C1182

World Geography Card

Ukraine

Capital: Kyiv (Kiev)
Est. Population: 46,710,816
Currency: Hryvna

Country Card C1183

World Geography Card

United Arab Emirates

Capital: Abu Dhabi
Est. Population: 2,602,713
Currency: U.A.E. dirham

Country Card C1184

World
Geography
Card

United Kingdom

Capital: London
Est. Population:
60,609,153
Currency: Pound
sterling (£)

Country Card C1185

World
Geography Card

United States of America

Capital: Washington,
D.C.
Est. Population:
298,444,215
Currency: US Dollar

Country Card C1186

World
Geography
Card

Uruguay

Capital: Montevideo
Est. Population:
3,431,932
Currency: Uruguay
peso

Country Card C1187

World
Geography Card

Uzbekistan

Capital: Tashkent
Est. Population:
27,307,134
Currency: Uzbekistani
sum

Country Card C1188

World Geography Card

Vanuatu

Capital: Vila
Est. Population: 208,869
Currency: Vatu

Country Card C1189

World Geography Card

Vatican City

Capital: Vatican City
Est. Population: 932
Currency: Euro

Country Card C1190

World Geography Card

Venezuela

Capital: Caracas
Est. Population: 25,730,435
Currency: Bolivar

Country Card C1191

World Geography Card

Vietnam

Capital: Hanoi
Est. Population: 84,402,966
Currency: Dong

Country Card C1192

World
Geography
Card

Western Sahara (proposed state)

Capital: El Aaiun
Est. Population: 278,600
Currency: Tala

Country Card C1193

World
Geography Card

Yemen

Capital: Sanaá
Est. Population: 21,456,188
Currency: Rial

Country Card C1194

World
Geography
Card

Zambia

Capital: Lusaka
Est. Population: 11,502,010
Currency: Kwacha

Country Card C1195

World
Geography Card

Zimbabwe

Capital: Harare
Est. Population: 12,236,805
Currency: Zimbabwean dollar

Country Card C1196

Made in the USA
Middletown, DE
27 May 2020